PRELUDE, INTERLUDE & ENCORE

DEBASISH MAJUMDER

Copyright © Debasish Majumder
All Rights Reserved.

This book has been published with all efforts taken to make the material error-free after the consent of the author. However, the author and the publisher do not assume and hereby disclaim any liability to any party for any loss, damage, or disruption caused by errors or omissions, whether such errors or omissions result from negligence, accident, or any other cause.

While every effort has been made to avoid any mistake or omission, this publication is being sold on the condition and understanding that neither the author nor the publishers or printers would be liable in any manner to any person by reason of any mistake or omission in this publication or for any action taken or omitted to be taken or advice rendered or accepted on the basis of this work. For any defect in printing or binding the publishers will be liable only to replace the defective copy by another copy of this work then available.

I dedicate This Book to My father, Late Sukumar Majumder and my mother Namita Majumder, without whose support and inspiration I may not able to write these poems and if anybody wants to commend my poems they must commend them as they are my only source of inspiration.

Contents

Contents

Contents

1. HEGEMONY IN PROGENY!

'Hello Dear hubby, I am conceived'
Which I expressed to my hubby with utter delight
He asked me, 'Dear did your hear baby's heart beat?'
I expressed with euphoria,' yes, I am enjoying its sound which
gives me a delectable treat'.

Heart is the only organ which first developed in human fetus
It alone enables rest all organs to ensure nutrients which is its
onus
It is the heart to make all organ to dance in chorus
For a baby to develop gradually in human fetus!

Finally I gave birth of a baby in due time
Baby's first scream alone declare its entity in nature's floor which
is prime
I felt extremely satiated that my endeavor and struggle ultimately
gain success
My progeny will eventually roll on with eventually with sheer
grace
It will bear the long evolutionary history of human civilization

*Where oppression and ecstasy both are entwined with different
jubilation
My aspiration is my child will bear the essence of humanity
Centuries long inequality will be dispelled by ushering sheer
harmony.*

*I wonder, who can translate
My baby is the only carrier of our conjugal effort with our behest
Nothing truly lost whether in the Earth or universe
My offspring is the eloquent testimony to carry out with a new
energy in nature's texture
But can I ignore the gravity of social fabric
Which plays a determining role for my cerebral to constitute and
explore
And develop with due design to reign in nature's floor
To promote human as supreme in galore
It too have huge impact for a nascent to grow as unique
Utterly different from the previous generic flavor with an
intriguing freak
A new matter to usher numerous changes in an available texture
with complex trick!*

*If a Meson enables to construe an atomic structure by sacrificing
its own entity
Neutrino too a product ignoring the status quo with its
adamancy with due authenticity
Giving a child birth is a grand phenomena of nature*

Where enduring huge pain only women can give birth to a new
life with ecstatic clamorr

But we hardly care of pain and death
A never ending phenomena only on Earth exist to bequeath
While giving birth
Myriad mother and their offspring failed to see the light of Earth
What a grand fest
But many are sadly deprived with haste!

Mother, you alone possess a grand role
Whether black or white hole
Hardly it makes any impact to human's social protocol
But mother, alone for you
We all are experiencing a fresh leash of life with grand hyperbole!

2. ENIGMA IN FALL!

Fall is a nature's intriguing design
Which actually trigger us to align
Fall is no longer a sign of disgrace
It alone having the energy and potential to instigate us to
embrace
Daring to combat all adverse force tend to malign
Fall is a colorful rendition devoid of fear from winter's invasion
Autumn in nature's floor arrange all carnivals with grand
expression
Bearing the message that winter is not the ultimate end
Subsequently nature will herself renew to herald a new form to
claim!

Fall is not at all an epitome of failure
It alone script in nature's floor with rich manure
Festering flowers and fruits falling from top to bottom after
completing its due tenure
Enabling to enhance the soils grandeur for roots
To express their renewed versions in shoots
Amazingly they all explore in nature's floor to brood
A new synthesis thus encompass our milieu only to ensure
delectable soothe

From top to bottom
An episode paved the way in nature's floor only to refurbish with
stunning blossom
A new leash of ife
With intriguing design and vibe
A continuity always emerge to facilitate evolution
Change appears as the only constant to usher the process with
due acceleration!
Rise is an inevitable phenomena
It cannot be subdued with any human imagined anathema
Soul even help to construe a story of stagnation and static
promotion
The only thing driven by an unknown energy with its
constituents to form a new synergy
Utterly being imagined by human's cerebrals unknown chemicals
to act intrinsically
To engulf and influence myriad exponentially
Hardly we poor souls of human incapable to fathom
How an abstract form of energy changing our configuration and
consciousness at random!

Our consciousness too an abstract in design
Being manifested by the reflection we receive in our cerebral from
external world to align
we human unable to comprehend
From apex how numerous realm in history decimated and
extinct

A new form and content eventually appeared in nature's floor
Just to eulogize the presently existing stature as invincible and
static in galore
Hardly we poor human could comprehend nothing is constant in
nature
Soul too change its mystic behavior
It is the matter which truly only rule
Its paramountcy we human could hardly and only tend to
ridicule
Which is sheer minuscule
Which is not obvious to us
Yet it alone script our eventual foray in chorus!

3. SYNERGY IN ENERGY!

Oh Meson, you are great

Dedicate yourself to transform energy

To construe in nature's floor a stable atomic synergy

Electron, Proton and Neutron

Designing a configuration with sub-atomic particles to form an
atomic echelon

It is only available in nature's floor in a stable state

We mortals only envisaged its very essence and flummoxed in
haste

Meson your sacrifice being scripted in only atomic configuration

Atomic nucleus being bonded by your holistic dedication!

The conditions favorable for transforming inorganic to organic

Energy plays the key role with an intriguing dynamic

What an amazing rhythm the metamorphosis of life flow like a
limerick

Perhaps infants can enjoy its true essence which certainly appears
for adults as esoteric

That is why children are considered as divine

The pristine essence they alone bear with ignorance, having no intention to malign!

The human's designed organization
These forms of energy which we human cannot fathom in our spectrum
Who plays the key role for such emphatic foundation?
Like Meson, a hidden energy
Plays the key role for such unique synergy
Though they are short lived
But their contributions endow us a huge gift
They may not emerge as brand
But they tediously work for a brand to become grand!
Energy neither can be created, nor destroyed
A definition has become a cliché, no need at all to be adhered
This is heuristically crafted, needed to explore for more advance outlook in rapture
Can we ignore the human's history?
Which is being scripted by humans own design of signals to translate nature's serendipity
Myriad souls dedicated to formulate such intriguing design
Human society accelerates with their own energetic translated rhyme
It alone bears the essence of another elementary sub atomic particle like Neutrino
Which too an elementary particle having no such human's crafted ego

It is having weak capacity of interaction
Not containing any such charge to make with other any instant
reaction
But having the only potentials with an unimaginable form of
energy
Containing the capacity to script the all lost form of energy
The people who dedicated their lives for human civilization to
usher
Human memory can recapitulate by the Neutrino's intriguing
nature
It alone produces a cosmic aura
To align with all forms of energy in the universe to make a
grand panorama!

4. EQUALITY, THE ONLY QUALITY IN REALITY!

I am gazing at the sky
Where birds are flying in high
Suddenly two of them
I noticed engaged to construct their own realm
Making their nest in haste
Not merely for their own shelter
But for their progenies safe haven in grand rapture!

I wonder when a bird becomes pregnant
How male and female combine their equal effort in adherence
How they could realize
Equality can only make a healthy vibe!

In human domain
Women though only having the capacity to give birth
But they are treated with sheer disdain
Where we only notice equality is in utter dearth!

Fetters are heaped on only women
No true respect, but being only crafted women as omen
To glorify woman is being treated as weak feature of man
Human society thus only welcome their own jeopardy with male
chauvinism at random!

Male domination and misogyny
Despite making huge cacophony
Still we love to buy
Vigor and strength of men are none to vie
Male chromosome use to play huge role to form blood
Predominance of its presence in human D.N.A. creates only
flood
Hardly we care floods only bring ruin
In an existing mechanism to go for oblivion is only genuine!

Can we ignore the role of heart
Love is the only tune which reverberates in mellifluous
How it only promote the necessary thrust
To remain all organs active and act in chorus
Provide nutrients to all body cells and parts
Love and love alone the only symphony of hearts
We need to ponder on combine strength in zest
Not undermining one from other in any pretext
Neither male or female is superior
Both only make the synergy with grand design in nature's floor

Without one the existence of human race
Will no longer bear in nature's floor any trace!

5. INTRIGUING HEART!

My heart is beating
To make me aware I am surviving
When I was in mother's womb
It is the only organ which first started to develop
Followed by blastocyst's pomp
In a grand ceremony
I descend eventually to nature's floor with amazing symphony!

In due passage of time
Heart reveals in manifold with myriad's entity which is prime
I wonder how some become cruel and ingratitude
How some express cordiality with generous attitude in multitude
How some act with vengeance
How many explore nature's floor with sheer exuberance!

Heart ensures nutrients to all our organs for their growth
Blood, the only vehicle flows to overcome all froth
Still how one loathe
And become inimical to many with vindictive note
Without heart brain cannot work

*It cannot command our hands to grasp anything to to act
brazenly in stark*
It too possess an unique quality to expand its essence of love
*Humanity rolls by dispelling all paranoia for mankind to
triumph!*

Heart largely being supplemented by placenta
*Which human discard moment it descend in nature's floor
devoid any vendetta*
Lungs started to act by breathing air externally
*Our internal pristine configuration largely being influenced
intrinsically*
*By its abrupt design of complementing each other with vibrant
symphony!*

*External conditions could promote huge reflections to our
cerebral*
*Combining of both we, a living matter explore with grand
carnival*
Though we try to deduce the external world in our cerebral
*But our consciousness is no longer a matter which wee could
display with jovial rendition*
*We amazingly possess the entire universe and its evolution in our
cerebral*
*The dual of heart and brain, it is difficult to fathom who is
supreme in its manifestation!*

When I am in the verge of concluding the journey of my life
My heart would only crave silence and solace distracting from
any jibe
I will be placed in the pyre
Hoping I will be longer being perturbed with hue and cry and
eclipsed by only fire
I will be disappeared perpetually with no apparent remnant
But the reflections which I have received while living will
remain imminent
It alone carry the flame to usher the progress for posterity
To grow and serve mankind for the sake of humanity!

6. INTRIGUING HUMAN HANDS!

I have two hands, not more
I have two eyes, not more
But I aspire to see more
Beyond my spectrum,
But capacity nature offers me restricted in store
Yet I have confidence on myself
I can appeal to many at random as long I can ensure my
existence
To make a little effort with difference!

I am a part of many
I wish to be an integral part of them with harmony
I endeavors only to pave the way for facilitating many
I enthusiastically extend my hands to support many with
symphony
My hands too follow my command
Which comes from my brain in my errand
I wonder if my hands are so loyal to my brain
Are they too play any significant role to design, develop and
configure in brain!

Different people perform different works
Additional values they produce to proliferate and ensure human's
supreme status
But different people do possess shape and size of hands
Their neurological configurations too designed to deliver
commands
Which enable them to carve a niche in the society they exist and
resolutely stands
Some uphold in the social fabric with exquisite skills
Some are focused to malign many without feeling any sense of
guilt
The discrimination of mental fabric appears evidently
It too enable to construct hands which is evident to construe
ethnicity
But finally it is hands which uphold humanity and protest
When it faces hindrances posed by only few hands!

With hands we give clap to express ovation
With hands we make gestures to discard any unpalatable notion
With hands we navigate traffic
With hands we disrupt fleet to restrict from any consequence
which is horrific
With hands we create paintings and sculptures
With hands we too build fly overs and sky scrappers
With hands we could make storms
Owing to our neuron mechanism which too changes at random
Right hand sometimes proclaims right is might

Left hand claims it is the tool to mitigate majority's plight
But it is ultimate the both hands tendency to build
Complement each other for making positive yield!

Hands could mend souls
Hands could decimate evils and its detrimental roles
Which only bring despondence to many
By using weapons against their own community without any
sense of rationality!

We do possess two hands
Left and right with its contradictory stands
Sickle, hammer, bow and gun
All reveal its importance by the assistance of hands
But largely being designed by the brain
Which navigates the human civilization to explore with unique
train
With hands we produce bread and cake
But flaring up of confliction starts while we fail to divide its
stake!

7. TRIBUTE TO BULLET!

Asteroids, meteorites and comets
Visualize in human spectrum with to configure human's
amazing tenets
They all are having huge impact
Falling on Earth's surface for human's to attract
A nature's endowment to enrich Earth's surface texture
A composite configuration being designed to reign on nature's
floor with amazing nomenclature!

Metals, minerals and even non metals
Largely contribute nature's floor with intriguing design
Numerous elements being discovered and determined by the
passage of time
Enabled to configure myriad complex constituents in an
emphatic style
Surprisingly all follow a consistent phenomena where change is
the only constant
Yet many subscribe to the view who claim they are only
proponent
Not able to envisage they too are the product of nature

Changing elements too inherently contain this characteristics
with huge clamor!

I wonder how since time immemorial few only capable to eclipse
majority
How majority being largely dominated by their propounding
capacity with sheer fancy
Gold, Silver, Copper and Iron
Changed our life and livelihood at random
Greed largely crept on us us, triggering us to garner wealth by
devastating all sensible norms
We are largely being enslaved and marooned by mere mundane
luxury and comfort only to conform!

But surprisingly we are only tamed by Lead
A heavy metal which plays the major role to produce gun
powder, ammunitions and bullet
It alone appears as champion
The only heavy metal eclipsed us
And force few to resort to intimidate many without an iota of
reprehensible diction
Lead thus since time immemorial dominating majority
Minority expressing their acrimony towards majority without
any sense of ignominy!

*Bullets are still now fiercely hover on us by its intriguing know
how*
*Majority surrender to its domineering presence in our available
milieu in a lingering cue*
*Accepting incarceration and even succumbed for its
concentration on minority's fanciful hue*
Poor majority forced to toe and and dance with minority's tune
For Lead's confusing commendable trait to attune!

*Proton and Neutron derived through a process and named as
Hadrons*
Oh! you are utterly different dear Electron
You are from Lepton family
Having weak interaction with weird complacency
Weak are thus forced to subdue
*Where strong interactions determine the crafty work of nature in
our existing milieu!*

8. DILLEMA WITH CLOUD!

Fight and fight till they are doom
A cry intensely hovers on us and consistently loom
I cannot realize who is my enemy
With whom I have been asked to fight with what fancy
Eye for an eye, triggering us to vie
It may yield for us to have only one eye
Light years will no longer be gauged
Human's cornea will surely deprived from its food
Without blood vessels its stainability and enrichment with
multifaceted vision
Virtually will be collapsed with perpetual transition
In fights thus only emerge to disrupt our inherent navigation!

Owing to human eye
We human can enjoy the entire spectrum and utter delectable cry
But nature's intriguing design of mirror image
The color at the bottom we tend to hold at the top with our fancy
for subterfuge
I am amused and bemused with seven colors

The rainbow in the firmament only draws my attention with an
intriguing agreement
Nature's attribution is unique with amazing hues
Nature's bounty we all enjoy who are also nature's product with
contradictory ruse
Surprisingly nature's products all contradict with its own origin
Fighting against nature is an inherent feature ingrained within
product's paradigm!

Cloud flouts in the blue sky
Bolt from the blue sometimes occur to bemuse us and warn us of
season's unconditional tie
Wind blows to navigate cloud without much roar
Sometimes it sway in a certain direction
Sometimes it float opposite to attract our vision
We too sway from one ideology to other at random
Not able to realize the nature's phenomenon and unable to
fathom
Oscillating from one pole to other
Our eccentricity only reveals sometimes abruptly with rapture
Not knowing we are beckoning our own jeopardy
Digging our own ditch with sheer disparity
Top and bottom are two stances continuously in a process of
changing
Law of inertia establishing its complacency in a phenomenal
rhythm
Change is a constant mechanism centuries long existing

*Various social fabric being changed and refurbished by myriad
with huge enthusiasm!*

*We human can realize the magnitude but not necessarily the
direction
Human civilization whether a scalar quantity, I too wonder
Humanity now being largely suppressed
Dissenters are subjected to state's atrocity and greatly oppressed
Everywhere there is sheer stupidity
Majority's voices being gagged by minority's alluring pretext with
cacophony
Onus from getting rid from infamy too lie on minority
Who numerous times shown the light of hope for majority with
utter rationality
World history being scripted to uphold their glory
Though few but their composition and configuration is still a
matter of quandary!*

9. INTRIGUING GRAVITATION!

I love to wander lonely as cloud

Going beyond gravitation and expressing my entity in loud

Hardly I care I am having resemblance as light

Consequently I go up with delectable flight

Still my presence too explicitly display my identity

I love to declare brazenly, considering the gravitation and its

unique entity!

Gravitation is not mere a subject of Earth and it exhibit its

overall lovely hue

All other planets in the solar system do hold their satellites and

maintain a status quo

Devoid of any dearth

It is truly a subject since centuries long to ponder for human

faculty and secured an intriguing berth!

Collapse in gravitation

Paved the way for solar system to evolve with emphatic

expression

Cloud of compression and dissemination

Enabled a system to manifest with mystic ramification!

I wonder why cannot we ponder
Planets existing in our solar system configuration are arrested in
an inherent chamber
Having innumerable satellites in astounding number
One is significant and striking
Venus revolves opposite in spin unlike other planets orbital
spinning
Unity in opposites do exist in our overall configuration in an
amazing rhythm
I wonder how gravitation plays the predominantly in every
planet to maintain an amazing algorithm!

I am amazed to observe the importance of gravitation
Where in planet Earth water bodies as well atmosphere
maintain a status quo in gestation
It appears as predominant with its intriguing rendition
Yet water, the prime basis of lives in expression
Devoid of salinity paves the way for myriad lives to express its
entity and vibes
Growth, proliferations and profits became the conditions for life
to explore
A new nomenclature emphatically claim it is the only way to
thrive in galore
I wonder loss is why only pave the way to usher for grave

Obliterating numerous lives being scripted by few with sheer
deprave!

I only wonder whose growth, proliferation, gravity and entity
We tend to celebrate to glorify for meagre privileged creatures
serendipity
I cannot envisage the other planets as well satellites impact
Eclipsing our sensibility too with sheer camouflaging essence
Magic, charm and beauty
These three emotive forces engulf us with mystic color and
complacency!

Cloud eventually confuse us and triggers to flout
Not bothering our entity which is in jeopardy and crying in loud
Our visuals are marred, impeding to bloat
Beyond cloud the gravitation becoming weak not allowing us to
float
Going beyond the attraction mechanism of Earth
There is no dearth and we express apathy to wither ourselves at
large
But I do subscribe with a view
Scantily, but it too exist in Earth's floor, no longer desirous to
adieu
Gravitation on Earth no longer becomes blur
Only to bemuse us to adore and sustain in nature's floor with
slur!

10. INTRIGUING LANGUAGES AND ITS MANIFESTATIONS!

Language and signals

The humans greatest arsenals

For mankind to express their vibes and emotions

Centuries long a tendency being crafted by humans endeavors

It too evolved and followed a process of evolution

Unfolded with their mysterious incapacity to translate their

mystical revelation

Humans are forced to resort spectra and its prevalence eclipsing

human eco system

How poor humans can anticipate they are paving their own ruin

and indulging only mayhem!

In present age languages have evolved a lot

In the passage of time it has reached to its acerbic intensity and

appears as a blot

which ony bears the testimony of entering to an age to rot

It too evolved and flowed in a process of evolution

Unfolding gradually in the passage of time to translate and

expression

Few eccentrics designed geometrical episode, paving for the way
of majority's extinction
Language gradually becomes a weapon to strike majority
Majority who are incapable to minority's dictum are sadly
unable to read their obituary!

Human civilization progressed and proceeded in exuberance
Where rationality expressed in manifold and subdued as a tool to
many with abhorrence
But we humans are only eclipsed with enigmatic expressions
I wonder why we fail to comprehend other creatures of nature
and their expressions
How they are crying and dying
Owing to human's tyranny and unrestrained orgy to garner
opulence at any cost to only malign
And obliterating other creatures sign and signature in nature's
floor with their inherent design
We humans are alone welcoming our own jeopardy
To the eco system where we alone thrive with harmony
We are scripting our own signals with sensational dictum
To produce waves for many to inundate at random
Loosing their capacity to judge
Majority are being submerged with sheer fudge
Thus humans are changing their languages in accordance to their
available circumstances
Which may fit only few to usher to reach to the apex!

But I wonder how long
Majority being duped by minority with their tune to forlorn
How many will find bliss
To the ruse of few such morons pernicious tricks
New language will surely emerge
Where myriad will find utterances and express their joviality in
chorus
Birds, bees and other creatures of nature
Will be allowed to thrive with grand rapture
To maintain a sensible eco system
Where human posterity could thrive and explore with sheer
exuberance!

Languages are being scripted in the sky
Who cannot read, those poor creatures will surely embrace death
and sigh
As they have no right to exist in any pretext to vie
Because of them only majority are subjected to sheer atrocity and
cry
Their heist on nature's floor
Only beckon jeopardy to overall mankind in galore
They only focused brazenly for mere profit and lust
Hardly they could envisage they are merely digging their own
ditch with haste
In nature's crust to respond for craving their mundane opulence
in behest
They unfortunately unable to decipher

Anew language are in the process to evolve to ensure majority's
growth with vibrant clamor!

Nature is vindictive by all means
For few who try to deceive and claim their superiority with their
ludicrous whims
Who hardly bother how solar system exist and evolve
Where alone Venus revolves in opposite direction unlike other
planets to conjure
The planet we dwell draws our attention at a glance
Hardly we majority could comprehend its manifestation by our
vision
Though we all have eyes but unfortunately we fail to evaluate its
stance
We sadly being confined in our dwelling planet
Not exactly able to fathom the cosmic equation and its mystic
facet
Which too influence our souls to construe our expressions with
our pride in vibrant tenet!

11. NAUTURE'S UNPREDICTABLE FURY!

Mountains, woods and sea
Continuously induce me to explore and enjoy the nature's bounty
with glee
Never fatigued I become
To enjoy the nature's endowment at random
Which I love and frequently resort to for enjoying a jocund
company
To get rid of city life's monotony and eventually align with
nature's eternal symphony!

But they despise me
Who are snatching the woods, mountains and seas with their
brazen spree
Mundane wealth, luxury and comfort are their only subject to
heed
They are ready to go to any extent to satiate their unrestrained
greed
Devastating nature and beckoning jeopardy to many
Poor majority are becoming the worst victims to nature's fury

Who are the product of nature
And feel comforted in nature's floor with clamor
Wink of an eye their lives would have been obliterated from
nature's floor
Majority's lives have no value to few eccentric's mindset and
design to garner only wealth
But they are busy with their pernicious traits, not bothering to
majority's fate
Not knowing their ephemeral lives in nature's floor too in
precarious phase
Hardly they care for nature and ecosystem
They only focus to cause mayhem
Still they remain unperturbed and unpunished
And enjoy their supremacy with an ego that they will never be
vanished
Only for few rabid loonies ecstasy and hegemony
Poor mass is paying the price of their lives and legacy
Majority alone are the motive force of scripting the world history
Minority's emotive traits only paved them to go into oblivion
repeatedly
Centuries long exploitations, repressions flow
But surprisingly in the upstream they successfully capable to
swim and glow!

Hardly the few can envisage
Reciprocation too inevitably evolve in due time to presage
Upside down is just a matter of time and space

Unicellular organism cannot follow the process of evolution in
any stage
Their greed only compounding to more complex rhythm
Where hardly they could comprehend the human civilization's
progress and its algorithm
Today whom they are burying
The day is not very far when they would get any scope for crying
When majority will bury them with ecstatic vengeance
None could extract from excavating their residual skeleton in
future for any reference
What was their regime and when they reign
To substantiate their supremacy and their esoteric claim!

12. ULTIMATE DESTINY OF CULTURE!

A farmer is ploughing the field
He alone reaping and aspiring
He will surely enjoy his yield
To satiate his soul with all his need.

A hunter is aiming to kill a stag in an unequitable fray
Predator and prey, a feature he alone displaying for one to stay
Hunter is an eloquent testimony of the most ancient occupation
of tyranny
Where a poor creature is at lurch
But in nature's amazing ecosystem having no grudge
Killing spree makes the hunter blind
Greed thus creeps among us
Only to justify our desire with amazing buzz!

Our culture, our creed only reflects our need
With an inherent disposition to maintain a status quo eclipsed
by mere greed
Ignoring a sense of forbid

We amazingly take fancy on our self designed sculpture
Where animal figure with human face amused us with rapture
Which only emulate our stature in nature's floor with grand
appurtenances
We cannot get rid of our self styled mechanism
Where anomaly in distribution of wealth is only in prevalence
To usher human civilization to proceed with persistence!

A continuity of dominance we construed even among us
We intimidated as well enslaved our own species with ruckus
Minority enjoyed delectable supremacy with jeering ecstasy
Majority being maimed and their voices were suppressed with
utter cacophony
Few may equate this irrational inclination as success
Not able to fathom how in future failures will script a new
definition of success!

In modern age
Farmers and hunters do exist and changed their strategy and
style with refined rage
Science and technology enabled them to sharpen their weapon
Where even without their physical presence they can reach out to
their prey
And killed innumerable with gay
Clicking of a plastic mouse
They can vitiate their available milieu which is extremely
difficult to douse

But when the cloud of their greed will disappear
They will appear discerningly with their mere vulnerable
number
Then they will surely be paid by their own coin
A coin which will no longer bear their regime and nefarious
reign in any side of the coin!

13. NATURE'S INTRIGUING DUALITY!

I observed a small girl in the street
Struggling to keep herself warm in the cold with bare feet
Seeking with many beside fire
Not capable to warm herself from nature's inbuilt attire
Where she appeared as almost naked
Shivering and following a gradual proceed towards an inevitable
dying state
Fighting against nature hardly having a faint hope
Survival for the fittest she unable to gauge with an iota of hope
Gradually she became pale and blue
Death finally engulfs her with its mystic hue!

While I am observing her from the cozy design of warmth
I am having no dearth to fight against nature and her wrath
In winter I have adequate measure
In summer my air conditioner keeps me in a soothing
atmosphere
Why should I lament for that poor creature

Who is incapable to protect herself from nature's rage and glare?

I hardly care of her imagination
How she experienced death and took stride on nature's
premonition
I am happy with my world of fantasy and imagination
Where I explore my world with joyous revelation
I am only obsessed with my cake
Why should I bother who are not able to afford bread?
My delight lies with my pride
Where nature seems to subdue herself to my championing ride!

I adamantly declare
I am supreme and who dare to dictate against nature's rustic
flair
Warmth or cold, never makes any difference to my behavior
I reign and explore with abundance of ecstasy with rejuvenating
flavor!

14. TEARS FROM A DAD'S SOUL!

I am truly bearing an excruciating pain
I wonder, am I truly deserved to be subjected to such disdain?
My only dear girl unfortunately raped and murdered
By the perpetrators who took the advantage for her lone situation
to adhere
She felt helpless when she was returning from her place of work
Where she work with her male counterpart shoulder to shoulder
without any dearth
Her upbringing and nurtured intelligence
She marvels out of her own wit to excel with utter exuberance.

Being a father moment I receive the tiding
My dear daughter is missing
While she was on her way to rest to her endearing nest
A sense of fear engulfed me, what has happened to her
Why she is not conveying her present status
I cannot restrain my jittery for her brief hiatus
Fear and agony engulfed me
I cannot decide what to do in the present hour
From pillar to post I am running to acquire her where about

Whether she is in bout
I am helpless, I am feeling dizzy
My dear daughter whether confronting any misery?

I never felt equal stress
When my son is outside even at midnight
I never asked him, why he did not inform me about his flight
I am rest assured he must be well secured in his coterie
After all we are accustomed to buy
Men are different and well secured comparing to their
counterpart without any sigh!

It is our available social fabric
Where men are forced to undermine female taking advantage of
their physical configuration
This is entirely nature's trick
Where men and women both are subdued to nature's intriguing
sync!

Suddenly I received a call from local police station
Asking me to appear before them with haste for certain
interrogation
I reached with my earliest possibility
Only to recognize my dear daughter's dead body in nearby
mortuary
Alas! Her mundane body being in a state of grotesque

Evil doers made their distorted orgy with a sign without any
purview
Which nobody perhaps can decipher with any clue
I only wonder and asked to myself
My poor daughter does deserve such infamy and disgrace?
Being educated she went to her place of work
How come she could be a subject of orgy of few eccentric at stark!
In the mortuary I am forced to identify her corpse
My dear daughter is no more, a mere body only in a phase to
fester and fraught
I momentarily cannot buy
A living soul can be silenced perpetually by few fanatics
nefarious cry!

I am upbringing my son and a daughter both with equal fervor
Since inception they are just child without discriminating their
sexual stature
I never conceived my daughter would be subjected to any atrocity
in future for her gender
How could I envisage the societal guidance?
Which may eclipse by gender biases to subject such heinous
affair?
In due course of time
My dear daughter will become a softest prey to such nefarious
crime
The perpetrators will mutilate my daughter's body

Whom I have to struggle just to identify with sheer agony!

I am now in utter quandary
How will we protect our female progeny from such infamy?
Mothers, wives and sisters
Continuously strive to render their utmost fervor
For them only we all dwell in this planet with grand symphony
In an available milieu with sheer harmony!

Alas! My poor daughter
Not she alone but myriad are now in flutter
Females are now becoming an endanger species
By males orgy they are roasting them by adding spices of warrant
They should restrict them in their house hold chores, culinary
affairs and carrying progeny
A middle age dictum we are now heralding with arrogance to
suppress their intellectual supremacy
I cannot realize are the perpetrators born from female fetus
How they dare to cause such inhuman ruckus?
People are now extending their sympathy
To a father who has lost her dear prince, clouded with sheer
agony
I wonder are they not a brother, father or son
Who are so impotent, not capable to care even their sisters and
mom?

I truly treated my daughter as my dear prince

I could not envisage queenly stature is no longer in existence
Male chauvinism has absorbed all fecundity
Only me like few fathers are left to shed tears for loss of their
dear ones surreptitiously!

15. BLAME FRUITS TO EVADE HUMAN'S TRAIT OF CRUDE!

Coconut is an amazing fruit

Amazingly it contains water in its root

To express its gravity with a rare attribute

When we acquire it to satiate our thirst

After peeling its superficial entity to enjoy our visual trust

We suddenly observe it too contains three eyes

Three in one, a nature's amazing equation always engulfs us
with sheer surprise

Nature, you truly an enigma

We merely bemused by the reflection you produce in our cerebral
with unique charisma!

Lotus too appear in human spectrum

Though roots submerged in water, but shoot express its unique
quality at random

Color it possess is truly soothing

Magic it produces in our cerebral with symphonic rhythm

Pink signifies we human are well

Flora you are mystic by your rendition with grand yell!

Banana is an amazing fruit too
It alone claim it is capable to woo
Though it is resourceful for peasants
With huge production it alone can yield huge dividends
It engulfs myriad with its capacity for innumerable yield and
sustain with exuberance
Poor people! They are deceived by its paramount quality in
nature's floor
Unknowingly poor human welcome their jeopardy in galore
Not knowing their entity in dismay with confusing uproar!

Banana republic is equally same
Where majority are being deceived by minority's camouflaging
flame
Poor mass being duped by its apparent magnificent essence
Minority thus exploit the available situation by their nefarious
presence
Though time and space scripts the grand episode
With utter relative sense it explores the situation in haste with
predominant chord
Republic though in nomenclature
It alone script the obituary of available majority in utter rapture
Myriad souls perpetually depart without making any significant
scar and uproar
What a fallacy we resort to fruits for our lack to gauge the
existing gravity
We subscribe to the view that perhaps it is store in our destiny

We blame nature is only instrumental to promote all anomaly
To cause disharmony to the existing human society to produce
only cacophony!

Gravity, anti-gravity, motion and demotion
All being mystified in nature's supreme expression
Three in one if we deduce by observing nature as static
We hardly can realize how momentum from beneath can too
having capacity
To transport water from down to up can yield huge fecundity
From root to apex with a quirk
When we know water as DI-electric
Hydrogen alone can make all the difference with sheer amazing
trick
Nature, you truly an enigma
From you only we learn quasar, pulsar and all other natural
phenomena
Things happening all over the universe with grand charisma!

16. FALLACY WITH AMBIDEXTEROUS QUALITY!

I possess left as well right hand
Left leg as well right leg in errand
I do possess brain with left and right hemisphere
And all are sacrosanct with their intriguing configure!

I do have distinct features like front and back
Top and bottom and left and right
What an amazing fabric
With a continuously changing physical sight!

I do possess charm and distinct color
I reign in nature's floor with unique flavor
My strength lies on overpowering weak
Enslaving many by my self eulogizing wit!

None can apparently distinguish
How nature alone render such intriguing trick
A tree with its manifestation by flowers and fruits
We only tend to admire its apparent attributes

Hardly we could fathom by a tree's apparent exhibition
Root and its expansion in nature's floor with what grand
corroboration
What a grand exchange nature alone initiate
Inducing me to possess more and more flowers and fruits to claim
supreme with prowess!

Many ideologies too emerge from our behavioral pattern in
nature's surface
Left, right and center thus continuously evolved with an
indelible trace
We thus get drifted from our focused agenda
Indulging nature to appear as champion by manifesting sheer
vendetta
Fighting against nature though appear as our inherent trait
But unfortunately we only encourage within ourselves to engage
in strife with infinite rage
Tending to use left and right in a single stance in chorus
Only to express a compromising tune to surge to keep mankind
in utter fuss!

17. DEATH OF INNUMERABLE MIGRATING BIRDS!

Birds are crying, they are dying
They cannot bear the human's endeavor of culling and burying
They migrate from cool to hot
They aspire to live with their lovely musical chord
Birds of same feather
Flock together with grand rapture
Alas! poor creature
How they could envisage human's unrestrained greed and
adventure
Which only trigger them to cause disharmony to the available
environ
Where all creatures in nature's floor are facing jeopardy in their
conventional echelon
And in the verge of extinction in galore!

We human love to fight against nature
It is an inherent quality we continuously encourage and nurture
Not bothering how we are poisoning our available milieu

Favoring few to exploit dividends from such hostile situation to
accrue
But nature duly take its toll
Causing disharmony and jeopardizing our prevailing eco system
with nothing to extol
We do forget that we too are equally nature's gift
How could we pave a discerning rift?
Enabling to extinct for many
Only to hear helplessly sheer cacophony!

Migration of birds and migration of human emphatically express
its presence
Both are conventional and help for ensuring the very existence
Color of variety and sound
Construe our environment which we only appreciate and
astound
A balance in the eco system continuously prevail
Where we human are part of the whole in nature's craft work in
manifold to avail
But surprisingly we human of late experience
Migrated labors too cried and died in nature's abrupt vengeance
A pandemic suddenly clouded us, where we felt utterly helpless
Lock down, a social endeavor we resorted to for our self defense
Not bothering how majority will survive
They only depend on their own labor to eke out and thrive
Culling of birds we resort to prevent us from deadly situation

*Killing of innocent myriad too we favor for few peoples safety
and greedy inclination!*

• 52 •

*Killing of innocent myriad too we favor for few peoples safety
and greedy inclination!*

18. FORTUNE'S ENIGMATIC TUNE!

I truly cannot understand what is fortune

How it acts on human with its esoteric tune

I came across in a play

Where Antonio, the central character, a merchant of Venice

Was in utter dismay for his unrestrained avarice

He was intercepted out of unknown danger in the high seas

His sails hoping to bring fortune moment it may touch the shore

without any miss

But, poor merchant unable to fathom the hidden danger waiting

for him in future's store

He was forced to experience the tumultuous situations in galore

Humiliation appeared as an inevitable tool

Becoming instrumental for causing disgrace and made him a

subject of ridicule!

From whom he borrowed money

Breaching contract with him only produced acerbic cacophony

The mony lender was only focused for pound of flesh

Which he crafted in his revengeful contract in haste

Only with an aim to bring utter disgrace

To whom who only claimed as superior for his racial superiority
with overwhelming brace
Forgetting who actually extend support when he was in dire need
His only confidence on him that he will capable to return the
borrowed money in due time
As he only belong to the superior breed
He will no longer betrayed by his creed
Unable to judge his future trajectory where money lender will
adjudge Antonio's crime!

But the law of Venice being designed in such a fashion and posed
in fore
Where taking toll of life against money was not having any
merit for making uproar
Finally after being tried and vindicated with vile intention
His wealth being forfeited and half of it was declared to be
entitled
By the person who was guilty of breaching the contract
Transformation of fortune thus evolved with its enigmatic hue
Engulfed the readers and largely being confused, whom they
appreciate with what clue!

Future itself is an enigma
We are utterly bemused by its charisma
It appears like an accident
We cannot comprehend its inevitability out of its inherent
constituent

Having the potential to manifest and explore
Where chance appears as a boon as well bane in nature's floor!

19. ENIGMA OF DARK AND LIGHT!

Woods are lovely dark and deep
But I have many promises to keep
Light is still enabling me to enjoy the ephemeral beauty in
glimpse
I wonder what will eventually emerge in flip!

I cannot ignore I am too in motion
Though it appears in straight line in respect to the available
milieu in correlation
I can discerningly gauge my distance from my desired destination
My promises are accordingly designed out of my sensory organs
accrued reflections!

I hardly can ignore I am judged by my space and time
I will be a changed version moment I will reach to my
destination
I will surely experience the transition of phase
Where my past will propound on me as long it will have due
interest!

I cannot ignore I emerged from dark too
My potentials are being kindled by lights intriguing hue
The light, which is the only food to my spectrum
Sometimes it engulf my vision with opacity as if an effect of
opium!

How do I realize
Out of numerous twist and turns
I eventually emerged from a mysterious cavern
Just to discover I am merely a creature of nature who can afford
to be hypnotized!

Still I appreciate dark
Which appears in my memory at stark
It only enables me to enjoy light
To cause deluge to my spectrum with delight!

It too vibrate
Making my sensory organs agile and reciprocate
Color, essence and charm
All appeal to enable me to comprehend its physical presence in
my cerebral at random!

20. HOW RITUALS ECLIPSE OUR VISUALS!

I am looking through the open casement
Dark night with dazzling light impacted to my spectrum in the
firmament
Clusters of stars
Attracted my vision with beckoning gesture
I wonder are they male, female or transgender
An intriguing appeal it promotes to my cerebral about their
mystic behavior!

Out of my alacrity
Many a times I threw stones at them with joviality
But the stones eventually fallen down to the nature's surface
Where i stood only to experience my grimace
It reached to certain height and subsequently fell down
Without changing its mass, it reappeared to me to prove me as a
clown
Law of gravitation only satiate me instantly
I rejoiced for its paramountcy which is my experimental prophecy
I admit its paramountcy

Which alone I concur from our ambiance with an amazing
symphony!

I consider gravitation was the only prime
Not able to comprehend universe and its amazing rhyme
How poor my own faculty to fathom
Electron, Proton and neutron and its configuration
Causes huge impact in nature's floor at random
The potentials of Hydrogen in water to suffice our existence for
metabolism and digestion
Centuries back there was no "I" to ensure my eventual comeback
to assign
How I evolve in due course of time to draw a sensible equation
of evolution to align!

I am a product of conjugation of male and female
But my existence not entirely determined by their emotional
turbulence
I myself is a Mistry
That is why I am enamored with chemistry
Not just quantity, I do possess a distinct quality
My progeny too will bear the eloquent testimony of such
intriguing ambiguity!

Suddenly I heard a shrill cry
My daughter who was experiencing travail, gave birth of a fry
Her screamed brought me to the Earthly realm

She gave birth of a girl child and encompassed her offspring with
warmth on her bosom
An aura of delight smeared and reflected on her face
Which I merely observed with utter grace
Male, female or transgender is not my immediate concern which
appeared in fore
A new life and its transformation I will observe to explore in our
domain with an uproar
Sheer euphoria eclipsed my heart with multiple layer
I wish she has born as a new star in my mundane star design
with delectable flair!

21. AGONY OF AN INTELLECTUAL!

A farmer is ploughing the field
By virtue of technology he is increasing his yield
What a boon science usher
To proliferate human resources with immense pleasure!

Three in one I observe in nature's floor
Soil, Implements and Human labor facilitate to make a grand
uproar
Three in one I do feel and feel proud I am a distinct breed
Computer, Internet and me comply a design in agreed
I too produce for human to explore
Not actually can fathom how I add to their well being in galore!

Yet I feel I am supreme
Out of my intelligence, which I consider only prime
I look down upon people who are not aligned with my wave
length
Whether peasants, laborers or other professionals who are socially
predominant

I firmly consider they are not at par with my intellectual prowess
and strength
Owing to my sincere endeavor only they are enjoying the fruit of
their yield in vehement!

I only can claim of possessing the unique idea
Which alone can navigate human beings with an intriguing
aroma
Innovations and disruptions are lying only in my D.N.A.
I alone can dictate the globe by my championing charisma
Wealth I amassed and claim it as an axiom of my prodigy
I audaciously declare
" I never appear in small letter", to uphold my megalomaniac
cacophony!

Abruptly I observe peasants upheaval and their outrageous game
They alone making gestures to eclipse my fame
They candidly express their intent and entity with vociferous
claim
"Bread cannot be downloaded from internet" is their only slogan
they adamantly proclaim!

After all I need food to eat and survive
People beyond my vision are truly struggling to ensure my vibe
I must pay my tribute to them
They are truly supreme and having the potentials to cause huge
mayhem

Disrupting my dispensation of life
Where I have nothing to feel proud apart from expressing my
vexation in jibe!
I tend to resort to a rhetoric
When I notice majority are struggling to eke out
They are desperately craving for equality and decent livelihood
I arrogantly subscribe, "If they are not getting bread
Why not they are going for cake?"
Forgetting that history repeats itself
Where my brazen trait will be considered as unpardonable
offence with rave
I will be obliterate in due course from nature's floor too for my
deprave!

22. ENIGMA OF CONSCIOUSNESS

I am amazed to see

How Red color smear the sky and tending to flee

Setting Sun is no longer making us fry

What a soothing scenario we observe with a delectable cry

Darkness will be soon hovering on us

We will no longer enjoy the beauty of light in chorus

A day will be soon passing by

Night will adieu light only to make us sigh!

I wonder the color Red

Which stimulate us to react in haste

Is it mere a color?

Or it only reflect the chemical expression of a matter

Its immense impact on human spectrum

Trigger us only to act with intriguing charm!

The reflection we receive from our in and around milieu

Having an impact on our cerebral with huge intensity to make a
rendezvous

The result of such intriguing proximity

Enable us to generate consciousness with distinct gravity

Nature is truly the only mentor
Who alone navigate us to make an emphatic presence on nature's
floor
Facilitating us to promote our signature
We poor creatures only eclipsed by our endeavor, ignoring
nature's lovely grandeur!

Our consciousness is not at all a constant structure
It too evolve, align and resonate with the nature's continuous
changing behavior
Landing on Moon is an invasion on nature's pristine floor
A new consciousness we gain and uproar
A distinction of gravity and gravitation we unearthed with
elation
Fighting against nature is our inherent trait since centuries long
revelation
Consciousness is too a matter with its distinct mysterious trait
Where we relentlessly explore to assign our distinct cerebral fret!

23. WEALTH AND ITS UNMITIGATED TRAIL!

Oh! I hate thieves

Who just paralyzed our social eco-system to cause huge hype

Hardly I ponder

Why they pose threat to our peaceful design

How they exist and align

In an available social fabric just to malign?

We construe a stringent code and roar

To punish them to suppress their uproar

Punitive measures we scripted and proclaim

We only are civilized who can only claim

To maintain civility in the existing social order and majority are emphatically blamed

Our measures are only sensible though it may unleash mayhem!

I still admire the old adage

Where theft being considered as accomplished skill, devoid of any presage

When one may victimized and arrested for such felony

Hunger, Crisis hardly make any impact to our cerebral with any
rationality
I only feel safe to dwell in my own familiar decorum
Where peeace only my utmost agenda to maintain a status quo
in my consortium
Where my fellow folks are in galore
Will extend their support to ensure my safety floor
I just feel comfortable to express my venom
Aiming to despise people who are inferior to me in social tier at
random
My class in the available social fabric
Makes all difference where I can only soothe myself with reprieve!

Hardly I glare at the inequality in distribution of wealth
Which plays the pivotal role to eclipse our sensible cerebral at
length
I belonging to the class of minority
My affluence and palatable lifestyle I enjoy without any
ignominy
My grace lies with my superior feelings
Majority are being subjected by minority's intriguing overbearing
algorithm
Centuries long a process navigated us to reach to the helm
Why should I care who are victims to my atrocious mayhem?

After all I am capable to buy majority
They readily acknowledge my superiority

*They tend to focus me as cult and imitate my attitude and
capacity
Poor people, they just salute me, ignoring my sheer mediocrity!*

*Unfortunately majority being captivated by minority's trap
Their freedom being snatched and are being forced to act
According to minority's designed map
Centuries long a sense of deprivations
Being glorified by unbelievable depredations
I wonder how deceptive design the minority still resort
By virtue of innovations, they hoodwink majority and maintain
their hegemony and clout
Human civilization spirally evolves
Where twist and turns only ensure a temporary resolve!*

24. PHILOSOPHY IMPLIES WITH MATTER!

I am gazing at the petal of a lotus plant
The water droplets on it attract my eyes
Its dazzling beauty caught my attention
I hardly ponder it alone grew from water's unique rendition
An aquatic plant of amazing dispensation
I only bemused by nature's intriguing expression
What bounty nature offers to me
I just enjoyed its beauty with sheer glee!

Nature offers exquisite expression
It's axis is beyond humans gauging capacity and exploration
Matters are simply comprehended by humans sensory organs
Sensations it produce to eclipse our sensory organs
We tend to craft a picture out of the image it produces on our
eyes
Which we observe in a stationery state, incapable to gauge its
changing trait and its vibes
We are comfortable to observe everything and familiar to
maintain a status quo

We are no longer aware, it just do not depend of our capricious
traits
And fixing all with our preoccupied hue!

Matter do create impulses to our nervous mechanism
Its changing phenomena excites our visual as well sensory design
We are largely eluded by its intriguing charisma and charm
An enigmatic rhythm always eclipse us and force us to make a
signature to align
We only can differentiate the taste of Mango and Apple
It do have the capacity to produce an impact to our taste bud
with ripple
But we are forced to restrict ourselves within a certain
framework
Without Mango or Apple, we hardly can deduce its physical
stature with stark!

Modern science enables us to understand
The Photo Electric Emissions and its persistence
How electron too excites To cause huge impact to our cerebral to
usher delights
Without switching on
We can observe the showers of lights in our spectrum
Even we experience the flow of water
Without turning on the knob of a tap to enjoy its clatter
Matter do exist whether we exist or nor

They do change and transform out of its inherent vibes and valor
which we cannot ignore
It is not just a physical expression
It is only an amazing configuration of inner contradiction
We hardly could comprehend the origin of all intriguing
component
And we too are configured by unity in opposites, which is only
resplendent!

25. INHERENT QUALITY OF NATURE!

I wonder while observing the crescent moon

The beauty it renders to attract out vision

Since time immemorial its appeal and its influence us in

trepidation

With its design and its gravity which was exponential

It has resemblance with the agricultural implement we invented

with our inherent potential

Which enable us to garner our produce from nature's floor with

its magnificence

We ultimately became settler out of nature's endowment

But can we ignore the reflection we capture out of Moon's

revelation

Which alone navigate us to explore nature's floor with immense

vigor and elegance

A crescent landscape alone contributed a lot out of it's

geographical contour

Which alone drew distinction with exuberance and at the same

time with majority's rancor !

River basin acted as the most effective tool
For human civilization to evolve with sheer misrule
Though initially it appeared in miniscule
Eventually it navigated and facilitated for few only to emerge as
predominant and rule
Making myriad as their slave
Manifesting their greedy tendency and eclipsing many with
much deprave!

A society being evolved
Where human beings alone can claim without any dearth
That they alone only capable to form a society to surge
Out of their inherent capacity to make camouflage
Within their own fraternity
They only can form a hierarchical design with conformity
Majority will be forced to align
By minority's capricious design
Creed, religion and traditional belief all will engulf majority
eventually
Where they hardy show any resentment to the traditional system
and express their apathy
Discrimination being accepted by majority without any uproar
Thus minority initiated to reign on them and profusely produce
a mist of acclaim
Where minority accustomed to suck the blood of their own people
without any qualm!

Since the nascent stage of human civilization and its exposure
The cradle lies on the crescent soil texture
Facilitated by nature's bounty
Water resources appear as gift to make a transparency
Unfortunately few hide the gift
Only to usher huge rift
Making opulence by depriving majority
The tradition is still surprisingly prevailing with unethical
occupancy
Against nature if we tend to act
Surely nature will take its toll for our recalcitrant protracted fact
Anything in excess is against nature
Can we ignore this truth in any form by our deceptive behavior?

26. GREEN AND ITS INTRIGUING GRANDEUR!

Green is a color of youthful and vigor
Trees and Plants display this color to satiate our existence and
desire
We breathe and survive in an available vibe
Precisely for green which is the only source for us expression of life
The only color with its pristine essence
Ensure our life and livelihood and enable us to thrive with
exuberance!

We along with all creatures largely depends on green
We eat and survive as well express our entity and grin
Though we possess blood inherently which having a color red
The only vehicle which promote the motion for us to exist with
rave in haste!

The cradle of human civilization and its grand exposure
Based on a landscape with crescent structure
What an amazing geographical contour

Which eventually determines our behavior and influences
attitudes
What an intriguing grandeur!

Our greed, culture, civilization and nomenclature
Largely navigated by nature's inherent design and intriguing
structure
It only enable us to produce
Surplus being derives in due time and possessed by few to adduce
They magically claimed they are supreme
Their hegemony are being the eloquent testimony
How brazen they are to promote their regime
Still this phenomenon is persisting
Where minority is dominating on majority and declaring
champion by their ecstatic cling!

We hardly could comprehend
Whatever majority may experience in vehement
Minority will surely topple us with their existing hierarchical
mechanism
Deception being the only tool for their long expressing regime
If food is the only source for our existence
Inequitable distribution of it only engender vengeance
In the leaf of plant
Photosynthesis occurs to substantiate plants texture and its
natural endeavor
Color do play huge role

Where molecules in leaf chemically react to light's intriguing role
Green, Orange, Red, they all play an important role change in
due time to complete a process
Finally, it is Green which alone emphatically express its
predominant role with magnificence
Myriad of flowers and fruits
Manifest in colorful gestures to express it's solidarity to nature in
gratitude
Finally it is Green which overbear on us
We hardly could deduce how it induce us to make only ruckus!

Red is the color of the vehicle we board
We exist in nature's floor and capable to make huge uproar
Though we initiate our existence depending on green
But the color of our blood is Red which only navigate us to reign
Photosynthesis is not the mammals agenda
Respiration only enable mammals to exist with massive
propaganda
Though we make clarion call in favor of green
But we never hesitate for our convenience to uproot the surface
covered with green
Greed alone we human perhaps only possess
Which only can disrupt our vehicle blood perpetually
Our all amassed assets can turn overnight into sheer liability
We will be obliterated from nature's floor without making any
cacophony
Where nobody will remain to script our agony!

27. IMBROGLIO WITH CONSCIOUSNESS!

I wonder, what is consciousness?
I, being a living creature
Always align with the changes occur
Consistently it forces me to adhere
Leaving no choice
In an available milieu
I only capable to adieu
The reflection matters produce in my cerebral to accrue
I only witness the grand rendezvous of inanimate and animates
with exuberance!

I do adore the image
My eyes are the only tool to make a camouflage
Which my sensory organs help to develop
With an amazing note it engulfs me like an envelop
I am captivated by its delectable rendition
I find true solace by its intriguing dispensation!

Nature alone is the grand source
Which bears all force

For changes to facilitate
Making new design to explore and proliferate
New one strikingly having no resemblance with its former state
Only capable to construe a new estate
In due course of time
A new design emerge emphatically to claim itself as prime!

I wonder mirage too exist
It alone having the capacity to hoodwink us without any resist
Nature is truly an enigma
Where we merely bow to her robust charisma
I am in utter dilemma
In between image and mirage
How will I perceive
Which one is real and which one is acting as an agent, only to
deceive
Both nature produce in abundance
Certainly in different condition to manifest its unique stance
One may act like trapped surface
Other enable me to explore vibrantly to script a new preface
Life rolls on in nature's unique floor
Where evolving of matters with forming a new state to express in
valor!

28. CREED OF GREED!

I am amazed with nature's bounty
How she endows her wealth to us extravagantly
Metals, Minerals, Trees and plants
Along with huge resources she offers at a glance
We thrive out of her blessings
Nature is a true haven for us with her inherent design to reduce
our sufferings!

But, few like me
Are capable to work as cork to restrict nature's spree
Gold, Silver, Iron and other ions
Even fossil fuel we extract from nature's bosom
What a grandeur she offers to us
We are grateful but we reserve it as the only boon showering to us
Enable us to dictate many out of our garnered wealth
Majority of us forced to believe
They do exist out of our clemency, which they find as reprieve!

Hardly we can understand
There was a time when our Earth has no such design to
reprimand
Greed was no longer in existence, sheer a subject of moribund

No vengeance, no chaos
All creatures in nature's floor thrive with harmony
No discrimination, no exploitation
Residuals of skulls give us the due annals
An ambiance surely beyond our present time evaluation
But a source is sure to exist
From where we evolved and persist!

Modern era only teaches us
Innovation and disruption is the only means to attain profit
We are encouraged to sing in chorus
Our self designed dream is the only tune for us to ensure our
existence
Which have no match to exist
We few only seat at the top
From where all wealth of nature spout and flow
Not allowing majority to enjoy nature's bounty and equally glow
Forgetting Sun never emit for few
Not able to envisage something ominous is going to brew
Unknowingly favoring a condition
When cloud of vengeance will overpower our brazen rendition!

The doomsday is not very far
I am wary when our cry will no longer be heard
Sheer silence will engulfed the entire world
Where buzzing of bees will also obliterate for few of ours
centuries long sin

*Our mother Earth will perpetually draw a curtain to usher the
end of all our torturous scene!*

• 82 •

29. TIME AND SPACE, A GRAND RACE!

I have three dimension
Front, Back, Up, Down, Left and Right
My fabric helps me to sustain in equilibrium
I am a matter being encapsulated in a design and being forced to
follow a straight line affair
Time unlike me only possess a straight and single direction with
its amazing endeavor!

I am a product of time
I enjoy a certain span of time to exist
Within a certain time frame I blow my might
I am a product of an unending process
Where nature crafted a design to produce progeny
An inevitable condition to ensure my existence and hegemony
Since time immemorial an unique design
Propound in continuum and inspire me with an inherent
capacity to align!

I only can make noise with a unique tune
I can convey my message to align with many to attune

Silence is nature's intriguing design to script obituary
I continuously struggle within my life span to uphold my
superiority
I do believe I too can make huge cacophony
Only to disrupt my own scripted design to welcome disharmony
I alone diverse into two
A contradiction I confront in galore
Where I encourage unknowingly to obliterate myself from
nature's floor
Without leaving any clue!

I born in nature's floor with distinct character and class
I behave accordingly unlike other human from different class
The reflection I receive is certainly distinct
Even I could discriminate from other within my fraternity out of
my instinct
How could I perceive?
What my cerebral will only reflect and receive
A matter's microscopic reflection
Only make furor in my sensuality and its apparent expression
Which nature honestly produce to enable me to enjoy a telescopic
revelation
I have no choice but to adduce
What nature enables to engulf my spectrum by virtue of its own
produce
I merely a product of nature with a distinct nomenclature

Fighting against it only endorse my claim as human with a distinct signature!

• 85 •

30. INTRIGUING IDEA!

I really cannot understand what is begin to grow
Germination is a process which is being applauded for its unique
flow
But we cannot visualize seed
Which is the only constituent to usher breed!

Soil texture is too a prime resort
Where seeds make their focus in grand exhort
Different seeds make different expression
We only applaud for its amazing manifestation!

If we consider Idea as seed
It too need required essential nutrients to expose with jovial treat
It may not visualize in human spectrum
As it manifest to engulf our cerebral with an abstract norm!

I wonder whether an idea is a human brain child
Its inherent trait are being inherently designed
It is the external condition which reflect in our cerebral to make
huge impact

Changing our configuration of cerebral with its style and stature
and tact
Which ensures few minorities existence with comfort and
composure
They may yield dividends out of their abrupt discerning affair
But poor majority who too possess ideas
But being discarded out of their inferior status!
I cannot rule out the existence of class
Where minority suppress majority out of their superior status
It is the idea which brings dividends for few
We majority tend to eulogize for its stunning hue
How could poor majority comprehend their mess
Could assess the colors intriguing trace
Red, Blue and Green
Finally dictate and dominate the matters sustainable regime
Out of these colors we exist and breathe
Innovation and disruption is a human devised charisma
We all surprisingly arrested by its construing complex expressions
in plethora!

Hardly we can guess
What exactly available in our vicinity and in what grace
Mistry, Charm and Color
Make the difference to construe all elements with vigor
Up and Down and amazing syndrome
Continuously acting to configure our design at random!

I strongly subscribe that it is matter
Which engender for all ideas to emerge in nature's floor with
rapture and clatter
But surprisingly majority subscribe idea as human brain child
I wonder how from human fetus emerge a healthy child
It too possess healthy ideas
Centuries long evolution has ushered the essence and gravity of
ideas
An embryo too possess constituents of developed notions
In the fetus it too receives the centuries long vibrations and
impulse
Necessity is the mother of all creations
An adage we admire with reasonable obsession!

31. DECEPTIVE SUCCESS!

I am in the pinnacle of my success
Sky is my limit, I aspire to reach beyond any limit
I hardly care of my designed ambit
I am in an insatiate state to quench my greed.

I wanted to become an axiom
I wish everybody would eulogize my wisdom
I feel sheer ecstasy
When in and around people consider me as cult to subscribe
their fancy
I take delight
People alone tend me to highlight
I soar high and high and high
My success truly get a sensible fly!

My success equated by my amassed wealth
I managed to manoeuver and manipulate people's labor with
brazen trait
My only aspiration is to acquire wealth
At any cost I ignored to bother

What I may eventually yield in rapture
My inherent quality is only to claim and overbear!
My only fancy to sell dreams
I cannot hear numerous screams
To induce many to adhere to my claim of false realm
I only persist out of their praise and hymns
I truly satisfied that many are trapped to my designed devise
Innovations and disruptions are becoming synonymous for the
sign of growth and rise!

I am seller of dreams
But I no longer desirous to buy others whims
I undermine others quality and innovative realms
I enjoy others devastation and decimation for their inherent
mechanism
If majority ignore to buy
I will no longer exist to vie
I am a product of mass exploitation and greed
From acrimonious and enigmatic fetus I emerge only to breed
With an intensity to force many to align with my designed script.

Three in one is my only slogan
By which I tend to show
I am successful and I glow
My existence is an axiom for many to blow
I hardly care about the majority's situation and sufferings

I only believe in my vision to glow which is only in offing!

I believe in three in one
The only protocol enable all to churn
From facing problem and to figure out and resolve
I wish majority too align with my clarion call for absolve
I cannot retrospect myriad Monarchs and authorities regime
How they decimated by time's tyranny and innocuous algorithm
Where disgrace engulfed their glory
A new regime evolved in due time to generate new form of fury
Hardly I could fathom in my orbital plane
At its center concentrated a huge memoir of various powerful
rulers regime
They exist in an abstract form
Usher a new rhythm to emerge in nature's floor with different
norm!

I do believe and adhere
'I' never appear in small letter
But vowels are surely distinct
Yet it contains the essence of consonant to vibrate and persist
Letters arrangement uphold the very essence of unity
Which paves the way for conglomeration of human to praise
humanity!

32. GALACTIC ENIGMA!

Cheers! an utterance stirs our hearing organ

Rest all sensory organs play active role

While we consume alcohol

An amazing tool we embraced with our traditional protocol

It triggers our cerebral

To reinforce with stimulation to make an upheaval

Celebrations are warm and persistent with immense heat and pressure

To rejuvenate our grand carnival with intriguing exposure!

Our brain is like an accretion disc

Two jet streams follow opposite in direction with an infinite tryst

At the center black hole enables to make uproar

It paves the way for galaxies to sustain in galore

Contraction and expansion two process always in action

Collapsing of any

May lead to sheer tyranny

Where singularity plays the discerning role

Our existence eventually go into oblivion with hyperbole!

Still being a matter we exist
Copied in our D.N.A. we evolve and persist
History supplies us in document
We cannot hide our inherent tendency of procurement
We may resort to supernatural power
We consider it as cult to resist our inherent glamor
It alone reveal in due tenure
How we manifest in nature's floor
With varied quality we conglomerate in quantity to explore
Only to usher time and space to make huge uproar!

33. ENIGMA IN CONSCIOUSNESS!

I wonder how a seed enables to form exponential growth
A tree come into being out of its grand episode
Surely it contains the quality
To exploit heat, temperature and pressure to expose its entity
No longer eventually we can visualize the very seed
We only experience its unique visual treat!

The external conditions are essential
To make such emphatic expression
Enabling manifestation of internal configuration
Light, water and other living constituents too help for a
symbiotic collaboration
Enabling a tree to emerge gradually in our ambiance
It is the prime source for our existence
Yet we hardly can evaluate its prudence
Indiscriminately cutting it we beckon in nature sheer imbalance!

We inhale Oxygen and exhale Carbon di oxide
We too supplement for its growth in abrupt stride
We need to complement each other

*Without tree we may may confront sheer predicament with
clatter!*

*Like in chemistry the presence of isomers
Apparently having no similarity and appear as misnomer
But it is the quality of atom
In extreme cool temperature it expresses enigmatic norm
Which we seldom able to fathom!*

*Like our consciousness
Where external world we sense out of our sensory organs its
essence
Without which we may not even capable to name them
Matter and its complex affairs make huge differences in our
random
Our entity too an expression of its produced reflection
Nature honestly draws her exquisite characters in grand
ramification!*

*Tree gives fruits and flowers
Which we can visualize in raptures
But it releases the most important element
Which alone ensures our existence in persistent
As we cannot see that precious element
Equally we cannot define our consciousness as a single event
In due course of time it too change*

*Nature's inevitable expression which we only experience with
joviality to amend ourselves
We only capable to capture her exquisite characters in grand
ramification!*

34. ENIGMA IN MOUNTAIN!

I am observing a lovely young fold mountain
What a bounty nature endow through its unique terrain
Unique rendition of flora and fauna
Engulfs my mind with sheer happiness in plethora
Color, flavor, Mistry and charisma
Upward and downward rhythm appears in grand panorama!

How could one evaluate at a glance
How liquid transform into solid substance to make an emphatic
stance
What a unique rendition of anti-gravitation force prominently
roar
Arrogantly express its presence on nature's floor
It is truly difficult to locate its center of gravity
We only bemused to observe with awe of nature's serendipity!

I wonder whether this mammoth mass appeared by chance
Or it was inevitable to express its magnificent trance
How could one comprehend nature's inherent rhythm

Which will explode in due time to manifest an amazing
algorithm
Intriguing features it too possess
Where liquid flow down from its apex for facilitating nestling to
access
Enabling civilization to manifest in galore
Human beings only exist to pay tribute to nature's valor!

I only helplessly experience
From my tender age how I evolve in a lengthy process
I am utter different when I became adult
Only to pay due respect to nature for my transformation, not
knowing her occult
I too have propensity to emulate nature
Where I crave to be treated as cult with distinct stature
Hardly I could envisage
I too pose as hinder to humanity like a presage!

35. CONFUSION WITH MATTER AND MIND!

I have seen a unique picture
It has blown my mind with rapture
I hardly care
Whether it is a creation of any professional or an amateur
It appeals profusely on my mind
Its impact hovers on me with intense wind
Producing vibration to my visual organ
Sending signals to my cerebral to make deluge
And force me to resort to recluse
I am engulfed with sheer fervor
I became a blind fan of such amazing creator!

I have experienced a mango falling from a tree
Hardly I could envisage in glee
How gradually the mango has reached to its extreme point to flee
I am just eager to have the fruit to suffice my satiate
No longer caring my destiny is intricately related with its fate
Only to substantiate my voracious trait
In due time it falls on Earth's land surface

It is the gravitation which proves its grand access!

Out of my sense organs
I experience the external world
Sometimes its produces grand euphoria
Sometimes sheer anathema!

Numerous galaxies exist in the universe
Amazingly all having black holes at their center
Perhaps the only source of gravitation
Scripting the enigmatic law of attraction
Lest galaxies would have been lost in an unknown direction
Where aphelion and perihelion
We hardly could gauge out of our measuring capacity of faculties
unique disposition!

I wonder what is mind and how it exists
How it expand or contract in what condition and persist
Is it too a matter?
The picture I enjoyed or an apple I observed falling on nature's
floor in rapture
How these distinct entity makes reflection in my cerebral with
immense gravity?
I am in quandary
Whether matter do have any existence to claim its supremacy
How could we ignore the very existence of matter's own primacy?

Matter over mind or mind over matter
A duality we hardly could comprehend by its confusing
nomenclature
It is the matter and its norms
We may not entirely capable to fathom its forms
Myriad stars as well particles never visualized in our spectrum
Still they exist and uproar on nature's floor at random
They play enormous role to configure our state and status on
nature's floor
Mind too is a matter we hardly can comprehend by its detour
Spirally it moves
Only to flummox us and amuse!

36. MUSIC REVERBATES IN TREES!

I am a tree

I along with my root always enjoy a shooting spree

Laves are my kitchen

They prepare food to ensure my subsistence

Photosynthesis, a process

Enables me to have an emphatic access

In nature's unique floor

I alone stand apparently and roar!

I am no longer lonely

Myriad of birds, bees, insects and other creatures

Consider me as haven with raptures

They never feel leery

No longer in jittery

In congruence they all produce a tune of mellifluous symphony!

They all breathe in haste

By virtue of my inherent waste

We both warmly complement each other

As their waste too satiate my inordinate desire
i love to grow high and high
To touch the sky above with sigh!

Though I don't possess heart
Still water being transported to my all organs with spurt
At random quark
I appear with colorful spark
I only observe with awe
How tide and ebb makes huge impact on me without any flaw
Gravitation enables me to stand
Anti-gravitation surprisingly helps me to breathe constant
As long as I may survive
I will produce flowers, fruits and aura with a distinct vibe
metals, minerals and plenty of constituents nature offers to me
with bounty
Plethora of twist and turns I experience in spiral design to grow
and enrich magnificently!

I only wonder
Without the help of external conditions and its clamor
How I could express my entity and render
Pollination is a grand process
Where external conditions enable me to manifest
I really cannot afford to have bliss
Loneliness is sheer disruption

No longer a resort for solitude, rather it may harm my
conventional amplitude
Against my identity and an adverse tool for me to exist in
nature's floor in gratitude!

37. CONFUSIONS WITH IDEA!

I need a glass of water to quench my thirst desperately
I never bothered whether the glass made up of what identity
Whether it is made up of steel, copper, iron or other constituent
I feel only contented as it satiate my desire in persistent
But if necessity trigger me to resort to glass
To protect myself from emerging scenario of fuss
I will surely use glass as the only tool
To use it as a weapon to protect myself and drool
Even if I wish to use it as flower Vass
To attract the attention of innumerable mass
An inherent quality always clouded us with with innuendos
Hardly we are capable to fathom our confusing crescendos!

The idea thus popped up in our cerebral and plays the grand role
The finest and the most developed design of nature thus enthrall
Human brains are the most amazing creation of nature
Which plays the key role for everything to evolve with rapture
Even enable all changes in the existing milieu with clatter
Nature's floor thus appear as the most fascinating fabric to
adhere!

I wonder whether idea is a chance
Or an inevitable gesture nature promote at a glance
Is n't it having a complex history
How we discard yesterday's glory?
How can we ignore past propound on us?
To make huge ruckus!

How can we ignore the existing process of continuous variation
of genes?
It enable to manifest myriad species at random rhythm
A new form thus appears in nature's floor
Engulfed many with its inherent mystery in galore!

How will we differentiate its quality and quantify?
A weird scenario we abruptly confront and forced to tie
A complex design thus continuously evolve
As long we exist in our orbital plane and revolve
Accidents seriously draw our attention
Chance gives us an escape route to claim we human are only
champion
We do possess a brain which enable us to capture all reflection
The only tool to overbear nature with jubilation
Trigger us to act in straight line
Spiral nature we hardly can gauge to align
Thus we experience always an upward and downward motion

Not exactly able to fathom our position, largely being guided by our pejorative notion!

38. ARSTISTS' TRIBUTE!

Oh! Ruler

Though it is evident you are a killer

Yet I cannot ignore your stature

You patronized me to flourish with flair

Because of you my art works being exhibited with grandeur

Gracious people acknowledged me with their precious rendezvous

to adore

They consider my endeavor as connoisseur's choice

They alone uphold their voice with huge noise

I must doff off to you

My fame, name and accolades are largely your blessings

I must pay tribute to your grand offerings!

To be honest, I love to retain a status quo

Where you and me both being complemented by the

circumstantial hue

Lest we both will be buried by the myriad's vengeance

A new design will emerge from the fetus of long suppressed

annoyance

We need to restrict such upheaval

*After all we only can soothe as well can retain and sustain our
grand carnival!*

*But your Highness
I beg to differ from your megalomania and malevolence
You are consistently deceiving majority
From whom you extract your royal juice to promote huge gravity
and hegemony
I would religiously support them
Even if they dare to cause mayhem
Your crafted devise of heist to majority
Centuries long an anomaly eclipsing such brazen dichotomy
If you punish and incarcerate me MeLord
I won't keep silence to align with your pernicious accord
I will raise my voice in loud
To encourage and dispel fear from crowd
Compelling you to abdicate your throne
To install majority's reign with a mellifluous tune
Only to prove artists are honest
They are capable to translate nature's endowed assets
Sheer inequality is the only reason of all retribution and unrest
And an urgent need of this hour to reset
Eliminating such vices from nature's floor
Humanity only can uphold its voices in galore!*

39. FALLACY WITH STRAIGHT AND SPIRAL!

I am a product of nature
I only having the capacity to express my awe and admire
Utterly engulfed by her endowed boon
Sailing my short span of life with her amazing tune
I sometimes feel gay, sometimes feel sad
Slumber acts as an indispensable tool to avoid her rant
An amazing gift of her to keep a balance in my secluded raft!

I do enjoy my journey of life
Not exactly knowing how nature regulate my vibe
Tide and ebb, a unique craft of nature
I only helplessly follow her dictum to bow to her mystic stature!

Nature induced all happenings on her bosom spirally
If we follow her intriguing design, we may not confront any
anomaly
But within me I carry a flame
Which ignites me to resist and go against her claim
I intend to move and act in a straight line

Against nature my efforts appear as abortive, still I stubbornly decline
My obituary thus scripted by nature on her floor with disgrace to assign
None perhaps will uphold my attributes in galore, hoping to only shine!

I wonder why I cannot become an axiom
For many to follow at random
How variation of gene recorded my past sequence
Contrary to what I do, nullify my very presence!

Against nature if we do not propel
I wonder, how humanity will explore and excel
Circle, cycle and repetition
Continuously itself repeal its order of stagnation
When we will fall on our toe
To act against nature only to ensure our inherent glow?
Lest nature will bury our all aspirations, credibility
We helplessly become victim of nature's intriguing caprice and serendipity!

40. ENIGMA IN DARK AND LIGHT!

At dawn, when light appears in the horizon
Dispelling darkness, it stimulates with a call of clarion
Birds, Bees and all creatures express its entity with wild raptures
Flowers petals offer with myriad colors to make a grand carnival
of delightful gestures
Makes a clear distinction between night and day
Rotation of our planer Earth on its axis makes a harmonic
display!

From the fetus of dark
Light emanates with its electro magnetic wave to stark
The only source in our dwelling planet to express its distinctive
vibe
In our solar system, light alone appears with weird trait to
ascribe
Which human faculty struggle to gauge with jive
By the reflection it caused to our cerebral to describe!

In our naked eye
Milky way with numerous stars attract our spectrum

Nature endows us with her intriguing tray
Hardly we human can fathom her inherent fray
What a spiral motion it alone construe
Upward and downward, a rhythm we only doff off to admire
and adieu
We are existing and observing such unique mechanism
A continuous process of change emerges with huge hype and hue
To maintain a status quo with an amazing algorithm!

Without the existence of dark matter
Hardly our existence could emphasized its entities in rapture
Gravitation and its persistence may not facilitate us to exist with
exuberance
Our entire design may not get at all any opportunity to express
its emphatic presence
We hardly could envisage our comprehension of reality
Which is a mere serendipity
Nature alone script our envious gravity
Dark matters presence in the universe enables light to express its
energetic flamboyancy!

We poor human
Takes gifts as granted by virtue of our own acumen
Not knowing how we are involved to switch off our existing
rhythm
Only to welcome darkness to engulf us with perpetuity

If not retrain our tendency to consider our cerebral with sheer paramountcy!

41. THE CONSORTIUM OF LENS AND EYES!

Seeing of a picture makes me sad
Going through a writing keeps me in delight
Music in my ears make me elated
I too amazed that I am composed of a complex design to claim
my supremacy with might!
I exactly cannot understand
Only out of my sensory organs
How I create a picture to withstand
Indulging to eclipsing me with extreme vigor and even
reprimand
Why I fail to evaluate the available surroundings and uphold
my sentiment
I feel regret for my ability
How do I know I am too a bait to malign as well align in reality
With huge design of conspiracy with ignominy!

Sometimes I wonder to observe with amazing rhythym
How unity of thought works with an unbelievable algorithm
How it alone possess the strength

To make huge difference at length
World history scripted with a recurrent changing phenomena
Where majority's voices being reverberated with intense
frequency, a delectable panorama!

I wonder by observing the minority's clout
They alone an construe huge cloud
Not knowing its speed
Only being triggered by their unrestrained greed
Beckoning their jeopardy, not aware of the characteristics of
speed
It too possess a spiral design in agreed
Where low, middle and high emerge with distinct behavioral
treat!

Three in one is a unique natural expression
We hardly can realize the nature's intriguing design and her
rendition
We human helplessly become her prey
Epidemic, Pandemic or other natural vengeance are being
offered to us in an infinite tray
How do we envisage her inherent design to emerge in an interval
to fray
Only to facilitate us along with many creatures to for perpetual
astray!

Still I acknowledge my existence and entity

Which is the only reactor to facilitate the reflections on my
cerebral with fecundity
Despite there are myriad episode to prevail and postulate
My sensory organs can only capable to capture which I
experience as supreme to validate!

Beyond my perception and comprehension
There are myriad matters evolve and express their presentation
They too have immense impact on my existence
Hardly I can assimilate their effects with my utmost presence
They do produce images in my available milieu
But my sensory organs cannot draw their pictures with the
nature's grand rendezvous!

Still I have a strong belief
My cerebral is a supreme expression of nature's unique relief
I do can afford to dream
To construe a new milieu with my grandeur of knowledge and
realm!

42. CHARISMA OF COLORS!

Colors and its presence
Having huge impact to human spectrum with unique essence
It do contain flavor
We are largely influenced by its resplendent glamour!

Green pigments are essential for plants
It enables photosynthesis to perform with elan
Without food none can exist in this planet Earth
Our existence will be precarious for its dearth.

Red is an amazing color
I wonder the creatures consume plants enable them to produce
huge clamor
They exist with blood which having the color red in their blood
The only vehicle they contain to ensure their existence on Earth's
floor in rapture
The vehicle which carry oxygen having the color red
To facilitate them to sustain with adequate nutrients and
validate!

Beyond seven colors
There are myriad colors
Which our visionary do not permit
But they do exist and emit
We are only allured by red and its vibe
It really do have strength to enable many activities to sustain,
restrict or thrive
A duality it alone possess
Amazingly it works to ensure our existence and progress
It plays a pivotal role
For plants to express its grand role
Flowers focused with myriad colors
But red plays the key role for them to focus
I wonder whether it have any relevance which they declare
eloquently
For myriad creatures to have blood with color red to express their
entity vibrantly!

Plants and animals complement each other naturally
Nature's devise are being displayed uniquely
Despite having difference in colors apparently
The rudimentary essence is to live and let live being resonated
equivocally
Red is truly an alarming color
Ignoring its gravity will only beckon jeopardy to the entire
ecosystem
Unequal dispensation of its energy and flavor

Will only script the obituary of all existing creatures destiny and their ephemeral clamor!

43. INTRIGUING DREAM!

I wonder

When I come across a proposition that everything matters

I exactly cannot realize what is truly matter

Is it only mere physical property

Visualized in my eyes with its mass value and entity

I am in quandary

How I am being navigated by its unique reality!

In my slumber

I dream of a dream

Sometimes it infuse me with huge enthusiasm in brim

Sometimes it engulfs me with utter grim

What a chronology it always activated on me to hover

It is really an enigma which always helps me to sustain with a cover!

I cannot experience atom in my naked eye

Yet I dare to vie

Claiming my eyes and envisions are supreme

It alone having the capacity to wage a new regime

Hardly I can realize
Before me my ancestors and their lineage
Playing the crucial role for my existence in nature's floor to
proliferate!

Matter itself expresses its presence with a crescendo
It appears with its enigma
We hardly can realize its charisma
Tend to observe in its absolute form
A contradictory character alone bears its norm
We helplessly eulogize matter as bravo
Not capable to envisage its impact on our cerebral in a moment's
go!

I cannot distinguish between dream and reverie
I am largely influenced by the external world and its expressions
cleverly
Dream certainly accelerate my momentum towards my goal
Derived from my brain, I habitually tend to discard external
world's role
Failures I tend to hide in an available protocol
Moment I achieve success to satiate my soul
Hardly I care of pains of myriad who suppress their agony
Failures how engulf them with sheer cacophony
I even don't bother success is ephemeral
I only become crazy to eulogize it is eternal!

I am too a matter with certain quality
Unlike other creatures in nature, I am capable to make my
distinct entity
Dare to fight against nature continuously
Not exactly knowing it alone creates my existence conspicuously
Dream is nothing but nature's honest reflection
In my cerebral it creates huge brawl in short interval
Calibrating my brain to adapt and adjust
Only to prove an invisible matter promote an impetus to make
me robust!

44. FALLACY IN FORMS!

Think out of the box
Whether a glass half empty or half filled is just a hoax
Either a box or a glass
A form just manifests with a class
We are tend to be arrested by its presentation
I wonder how form engender a conundrum and hypnotize us
with jubilation
Hardly we can gauge and apprehend
How form abruptly could be changed
A glass can be used as weapon
To attack one whom we consider as enemy with ample reason
Myriad mayhem too happen in nature's floor
Where form being eclipsed by content to make ruckus in galore!

When my act produce huge uproar
My heart started to beat profusely and equally roar
How could I suddenly comprehend
It is the only organ first started to develop in the fetus with furor
To enable other organs to develop gradually with adequate
nutrients to eventually focus

Attraction and contraction, a process always mutually works to
maintain a due status
Status quo a state we all love to sustain
Glass, box and various forms we adore and equivocally try to
retain!

Matter and its existence appears at random
Makes huge impact to human spectrum
Its entity alone reflects on our eye
Nature's precinct arrests us where we hardly have any option to
vie
We are forced to be arrested whether in glass or box
Alas! How could we judge we too are nature's prey
Matter alone creates an enigma where we hardly have anything
to say
We only designed to abide nature's dictum
A continuum alone makes all difference at random!

45. INTRIGUING HUMAN SENSES!

We human are amazing species
Out of our sense organs we exploit the nature's edifice
Yet we cannot fathom
How our sense organs play the crucial role at random
How it enables us to comprehend an available milieu in a
rhythm
What a grand offering nature endow to us to ensure our existence
with her whim!

When I explore forest floor
Myriad tress with variety of fruits and flowers manifest on her
ferny floor
The sound of leaves shivering
Falling fruits making decent noises on her bosom, which draw
an impact to my hearing!

But a flower with its stunning color
Attracts most with its soothing flavor
I could evidently discriminate its emphatic presence
Ignoring all in and around for my abstract fancy

Clouded with an inexplicable emotion with exuberance
My concentration hovers on it
To make it excellent to my vision which too is being restricted,
cannot further proceed!

Though nature has dispensed the environs with wide array
But not compelling me to confront an instant bizarre
Not knowing is it a design of self deceit
But for the time being it appears as exquisite and makes me
jovial
Nature's realm thus eclipse my inherent sensory device with grand
carnival!

I wonder who am I
Am I not a product of nature too
How I have acquired my nomenclature
How can I claim I am supreme in stature
A continuous process of evolution has shaped my present being
Whether war, epidemic or any natural catastrophic flaming
I captured and retained my entity
Which has only favored my own gravity
The process of capturing the available scenario in my cerebral
My sensory organs do play the championing role with favored
validation
Supporting my claims with exuberance
No other creature can uphold vibrantly to beat their own drum
with such intense pitch

None can translate such expressions as 'mind' eloquently to make a grand reach!

46. INTRIGUING ODYSSEY IN THE WOOD!

I am trodden through the wood
Bewildered by the beauty nature endowed
Equally it triggered me to brood
But mellowed by soothing scenario nature offers with grandeur
Dark, deep wood is a sheer fancy
Induced me to explore its stunning floor with expediency!

Suddenly I noticed a bifurcation of my trodden path
I am in dilemma which path I will chose to satiate my soul's
search
There is a clear choice being offered by nature in abrupt noise
I opted one and explored with a spirit to rejoice
Enjoying the beauty nature offers with serenity
Only to soothe my soul with sheer ecstasy!

When I realized my destination to a certain place
Where people are dwelling with utter grace
I cannot rule out I am a social being too
I crave company of my species with warm hue

The people I confronted asked me where I intend to go
I just retaliate, I love their warm company and flow
They welcomed me and asked with amazement
When they come to know my traveled path and nature of
amusement!

They inquired me with utter surprise
Why did n't I chose the other path in what surmise?
I myself felt bemused
As I could not fathom my own apprehension, option and recluse
I failed to envisage
There could be a life endangering episode to emerge with
vengeance
I exactly cannot fathom
My instinct do possess a rhythm at random
Navigating me to reach to my safe haven in nature's floor
I truly do not know any such comprehending roar
How my instinct would marvel to ensure my entity in nature's
floor!

Being a minute creature in this vast universe
How could I observe the plasma state and its stature in terse?
Which only absorb cold and release hot waves
To ensure life on Earth with myriad form and grace!

How could I truly envisage?
I am presently walking over a volcano

Which can erupt at any time, a living inferno
By mere religious discrimination
My dear country could be torn with vile propagation
What a dirty presage!

Ultimately it is the human life which will be only sacrificed
But I wonder in what aim and in what surmise?
My head is spinning
Not in half integer, but in full swing
The motion and its inherent rotation
I myself cannot restrain its impact on me in apprehension
Though I am always in favor of mankind
Which only can save humanity with a purpose to bind.

Really I started to believe
My inherent capacity is only having the capacity to bring relieve
I do not know what matter plays the key role
To its best to make utterances for humanity with a desperate
protocol!

I only wonder how I am arrested with an intriguing phenomena
Where my brain plays the striking role to dispel all anathema
Taking the apt judgement finally
The road I eventually opt to ensure my safety
Revealing the enigma being designed by human brain
Where I wonder external conditions play any pivotal role to
claim!

47. MERCHANTS' INTRIGUING MENDACITY!

Merchants are brazen, only crazy to focus on lucre
Though they resort to imitation in generosity which is actually
not in their genre
By displaying their flamboyant expression of hypocrisy
They allure many
Dazzled myriad with their ostentation
They are undoubtedly adept to display their malicious rendition
With huge hue and cry, they only capable to promote sheer
travesty
In an available social milieu which is their only U.S.P.
They are able to make majority gullible and duped them
Since centuries long we majority only witness utter mayhem
They never drift from their core agenda
Where profit and self interests of few they uphold with mystic
criterion
They adroitly execute their vendetta
Where they skillfully construe a state character to satiate their
vicious aspiration with bemusing charisma!

Even in Shakespeare's Play
Merchant of Venice brazenly display
Resorting to racial ploy
Ignominy they only express with nefarious coy!

Surprisingly in the trial scene
How a Venetian merchant being defended by a young lawyer to
uphold merchant's glory without grim
Resorting to arguments with a confusing expression to uphold
attribute and glory with infamous rhythm
Where the accused being flummoxed and ruined by defendant's
infamous mechanism
We audience are just blown out of proportion by young lawyer's
pseudo rational hoodwinking style in flamboyancy
Where reasons take backseat to eulogize the accused merchant's
religious supremacy and identity with fallacy!

When a plaintiff finally being concluded by the trial court as an
evil-doer
The dice suddenly change the climax where a money lender
Though a businessman forced to accept the devise being crafted
by few who are truly the game changer
The plaintiff being unfortunately accused of only responsible to
act the guilt
Primarily being driven by religious doctrine adverse to the
opponent to make a tilt
Forcing him to declare as bankrupt

By confiscating all his belongings with a false texture
Sanitizing him by not giving any opportunity to survive with
rapture!
Religious persecution is not merely recent trend
It was being used as a tool since centuries long in prevalence
Not allowing one to suffice, forcing to subdue to a confronting
malice
What a perjury we experience in a nefarious ploy
Not able to gauge that it only sustain in the social fabric like a
perilous toy
Where perfidy surprisingly wins our hearts
We unfortunately sway in gay, not able to envisage its
tormenting episode to cause only ruckus!

Alas! we are eclipsed with dearth of reasons
Religion only becomes the overbearing tool to blur our visions
Eventually we take pleasure, not comprehending we are
furnishing few greedy's goal
How ruthless state's endeavor which only pervades with a cloud
to engulf majority's souls!

Pound of flesh or mound of soil
Forest's ferny floor or rivulets expressive movements in coil
Nature's endowment to majority being ignored
Minority erupts with their venom to assimilate nature's all
bounty

Their unrestrained caprice having no limit just to claim their
paramountcy
They legitimize all their claims with huge clamor
Poor majority! they are utterly helpless as they lack glamour
Minority capable to influence the design of social fabric with
epiphany
Where majority merely treated as redundant for minority's
tactical symphony!

Poor minority, I feel pity on them too
They too are not capable to fathom the evolution of species which
act as the only glue
Where the new one having no resemblance with the former
From where they derive and evolve, devoid of any simile or
nomenclature
From quality a new quality always derive with a new entity
Which only heralded by nature with a honest reflection and
serendipity
People's knowledge we hardly comprehend
It is beyond the purview of human existence
It only carries the matter which transformed by temperature,
pressure and inherent design of nature
What a unique craft work nature alone construe
Where human endeavors have any conscious effort to do!

Economic design is the key of social fabric
Where exploitation by minority towards majority is just systemic

It alone produce all tricks
Where religion, philosophical or political doctrines are just
gimmick
Only aiming to ensure a state character
To maintain a status quo of sustaining exploitative nature
I wonder how we helplessly forced to align with reflection of
nature
Beckoning our own jeopardy by tending to bury humanity
without any sensible signature!

48. ENIGMA IN NATURE!

Woods are lovely, dark, deep and green
It triggers me only to dream
I love to recluse in nature's bosom
To renew my energy with a fresh leash of air at random
Where the bliss of solitude I enjoy immensely
I cannot rule out the strength of greenery
Which alone script an amazing synergy!

I hardly could fathom
What I observe at random
It is the tree Eucalyptus which are engulfing me
The lovely aroma it produces to make me glee
How I could realize
Myriad of such trees too endangering numerous lives
The poor foresters who are only considered as men of soil
Who only exist out of their toil
Forests only ensure their livelihood
To pose threat to them is a sheer brazen attitude
Observing them closely and their menace
I felt really ashamed

For few inhuman souls and their unrestrained greed to facilitate
such mayhem!

The area where the tree Eucalyptus being sowed abundantly with
ruckus
To make the environment green is the call many are forced to
become vociferous
Water gradually on that area becoming scarce
Human habitation are merely exist to cause a sheer farce
They will be eventually forced to evacuate
Few brazen wealth seekers are consistently eying and instigating
them to evacuate
They are only aiming to extract minerals
Only to satiate their crave for wealth which is eternal!

Poor forest dwellers
Their freedom being snatched by few megalomaniacs
They hardly could envisage
Numerous tyrants in the passage of time just decimated
The toil of foresters, their pain and sufferings
Will surely yield rich dividends to discard such inequitable
affairs and overbearing.

Trees are amazing out of their expressions in nature's floor
They alone help us to manifest in galore
They can change the nature's floor and its soil texture

Hardly we could comprehend why from the same soil fruits of
different taste
Allure our taste bud with enigmatic flavor in haste
As seasons are quickly change in respect to the space and time
But nature remain constant with its changing hue which is
prime!

49. FENCES ARE NEEDED TO BE BROKEN WITH HASTE TO SAVE HUMANITY

Making fences might engender our ego

We are isolated from many whom we consider inferior and low

We construe our own domain

We are contented by our own blowing fame

Fences, we consider as a unique devise

Being segregated from many out of our own caprice

Hardly we care

Myriad render their services for few peoples superior state and
soothing affair

We love to enjoy our higher echelon

Human labor we exploit, yet we tend to ignore their
contribution on our superior domain

Whom centuries long we conquered and made captive and forced
them to act as slave

In modern era we purchase their labor and transform them into
slave with deprave

*Making fences to discriminate them from our domain has
become our latest fancy
We few stubbornly adorn our own world where 'trespassers will
be prosecuted' a slogan of few became expeditiously!*

*We are now captured with a new phenomena
Where work from home being stimulated many with sheer
panorama
Though funny, yet many are engulfed with an amazing
syndrome
I wonder, Is not it a pernicious ploy to hoodwink many at
random?*

*Labor is the prime basic condition
Which alone accelerate and ensure the pace of world history for
its existence
As well persistence with jubilation
We may not perhaps have any opportunity without its
accumulated rendition
I wonder, how can we undermine labor
To arrest them and ignore their valuable appreciation
Discarding labor and undermine its supreme value is a crime
Which alone pave the way towards mortuary
Not knowing who will script the majority's obituary!*

Alas! we forget to celebrate

Association and conglomeration is the only key we need to re calibrate
United we stand, divided we fall
An adage being popular centuries long
Fences are just mirage
To confuse may and make us disarray only to produce haze
We need to comprehend the watery affair
Which alone enable us to visualize all through our eyes with adroit behavior
Water alone act as the sole ingredient, source of huge energy
Whether human brain or eyes, it alone draw the due difference with synergy
Breaking all barriers, crossing all impediments
Expanding our horizon with grand exuberance
Fences should be discarded as it makes neighbors as enemy
Huddle, Puddle, Cuddle and Love, the only path to rejoice and uphold humanity.

Good fences make good neighbor
We are largely influenced by its clarion confusing call and clamor
Continuously we struggle
How to suppress our own fraternity and put a muzzle
Force them to act according to few peoples caprice
Majority being throttled, forced to put their feet in few peoples shoe
Where majority collectively lost their flavor and hue

What a disgrace we observe in our existing milieu!

We few take delight for being segregated from many
Indulged to make fences even within our own family
It has become our utmost testimony
We largely being carried away by our own designed fancy
We are supreme as human, though restricted within few
Yet we tend to display brazenly out hegemony with ecstasy with
few trusted crew
But we should not forget the difference between Acid and Base
Which alone causing huge furor and posing sheer menace
Mankind is now facing utter despondence
It is almost at the brink where greed only working with a
blindfold appearance!

50. PATH, WE FORCED TO SEARCH!

The path being less chosen
Triggers many to ponder
Why it has been discarded?
Why majority opted the path largely being trodden?

Is it the lesser
Whom we love to level as loser
To celebrate in ecstasy
Endorsing majority as sensible out of our own fancy?

My only concern about the path
Which enable me to trod with abrupt search
I wonder the faith which induce many to to explore
No longer trigger me to implore
As I already align with many to trod
Making a choice of my own aligning with many to enjoy my
tentative episode!

Is it the path which make huge appeal to our cerebral
The reflection we receive to make huge carnival?

But I wonder the path we lesser trodden
Are they designed only to bemuse us for not being largely chosen?

We know that if water being heated
Certain molecules will depart in gaseous state
Will we consider those molecules
Their fate being destined to enjoy such minuscule?
Capricious nature having no intention to cause harm to any
creature
But out of its proclivity, which is its usual behavior
Myriad obliterate within a wink of an eye
How will we guess, why and with whom to vie?

It is the nature which actually dictate and dominate
We have no choice apart from following its design to imitate and
reciprocate
Is n't it the nature which alone appeal
We are forced to accept many, due to our cerebral, try our best for
many to repeal
It is our continuous process to fight against nature
To make amenable our milieu with ecstatic gesture
Still we cannot rule out we need miles to go
To force nature docile in terms of our intellectual flow!

Still I love to stick to my opted path
Though it appears in dissect, but I chose to enjoy my exploring
touch

At least I need to survive
I cannot indulge to suspend myself in a trough
For unknown to devour to script my obituary graph
Moving is the only process to ensure change, the only constant
Human civilization alone accelerates to serve mankind to a large
extent.

My only request to the modern intelligentsia
Please don't confuse mass to be hooked with paranoia
They might consider as an axiom to follow
Just to invite a doomsday by accepting your view which is sheer
hollow
Few eccentric will soon exercise their tyranny
Only to resort to a means to avoid their own crisis with
cacophony
But I do have a faith on a crisis point
Which only enable to form a new matter in new fold in
exuberant!

51. BATTLES OF BOUQUET AND BOOKS!

Flowers with myriad hue
Always makes us jovial
When It started to fester
Only to increase the fertility of soil nature's floor in rapture
Though the obituary of flower being alone crafted by nature
Where the ephemeral grandeur obliterated by its existence in
quick departure
But it enables plants to thrive more in future with vigor
Only to ensure its continuity with unique flavor!

Our tendency being designed by nature
Where we carry bouquet to satiate our fraternity with amicable
gesture
It has become our attribute
To offer bouquet, whether in nuptial, felicitation or demise with
grand tribute
But how can we forget
The reflection we receive from nature makes indelible mark in
our mindset?

It is we who admire colors
Which nature bestow to navigate our trait and statures
But we human having a sense beyond reflection
Which alone can script our received reflection in innovative
inscription
From where we derive our distinct design
Books we eventually invent to translate our wisdom in the
passage of time
Thus human civilization progressed with grand triumph and
jubilation
Only to prove human beings are only entitled to be accepted as
supreme and champion
To overbear nature by continuously striving
Our attire alone bears the testimony we are continuously fighting
against nature
To only establish we are truly supreme to justify our
nomenclature!

Flowers when drop from tree
It loses all its glamour and natural glee
Flowers with myriad hue and amazing appraisal
Always makes us jovial
We are delighted by our visual treat
How could we envisage our eyes are too nature's unique gift?
To soothe our souls

Nature's inherent music makes indelible impact to our hearts in
manifold
Truly the bounty nature endow to us
Enables us to refresh our mind in chorus!

But books are purely human endeavor
Which is the only tool to evolve our prosperity
Alas! we are now tending not to express our solidarity
Which alone is the only friend to give delight to us perpetually
Even when we are in a state of solitary
We are nowadays not fatigued to carry bouquet
Whether in fanciful ceremony or in plaintive company
Discarding books and accepting floral tribute has become our
ornamental trait
Which only bears our emotional attribute in haste
When we know that emotions cause only riot to our reasons
Still I wonder, how we are forced to be arrested in nature's
treason
Where our ability to think are being eclipsed
How could we indulged to be carried away by nature's deceiving
trick?

Becoming numb and follow nature's whims blindly
We are unknowingly beckoning our own jeopardy
Only to facilitate our ruin
Centuries long civilization will turn into relic, not bothering our
conscious endeavor and dreams!

Wink of an eye we will be perpetually decimated by nature's
intriguing trick
What a mystic blow
From big bang to black hole only restrict our natural flow
No Colosseum, no museum will eventually exist
To represent our acumen as supreme in this planet
Devastation and destruction we human alone can ensure
To script our glory as well gory in nature's floor!